Life in the Ancient World

Trade and Commerce in the Ancient World

Crabtree Publishing Company

Contributing authors: Paul Challen, Shipa Mehta-Jones,
  Lynn Peppas, Hazel Richardson
Publishing plan research and development:
  Sean Charlebois, Reagan Miller
  Crabtree Publishing Company
Editors: Kathy Middleton, Adrianna Morganelli
Proofreaders: Kathy Middleton, Marissa Furry
Editorial director: Kathy Middleton
Photo research: Katherine Berti, Crystal Sikkens
Designer and prepress technician: Katherine Berti
Print and production coordinator: Katherine Berti

Cover description: Leptis Magna (top right) was a leading city and
major trading post of the Roman Empire. Travel by domesticated
camels (bottom right) has been happening for thousands of years.
The Silk Road (bottom) is a famous trade route that spans from
China to the Mediterranean Sea. Black figure pottery (left) became
popular in Ancient Greece between the 7th and 5th century B.C.
Vikings made replicas of coins from other nations (top left) when
they started to trade.

Title page description: Due to the camel's ability to handle harsh
desert climates, camel trains were a slow but secure means of trade
and transportation between towns.

Photographs and reproductions:
Art Resource: iHIP/Scala: page 9 (bottom)
Bridgeman Art Library: Shinagawa: departure of Daimyo/
  Fitzwilliam Museum, University of Cambridge, UK: page 25
iStockPhoto.com: page 16 (right)
Corbis: pages 12, 20; Bettmann: page 21 (top); © National
  Geographic Society: page 26 (left)
Corel: page 3
Wikipedia Commons: Bjørn Christian Tørrissen: page 8 (bottom);
  World Imaging: page 11, 13 (top), 17 (bottom), 29 (top right); 31
  (coins); The Oxford Encyclopedia of Ancient Egypt: page 14
  (bottom); Karelj: page 22 (top); NobbiP: page 28 (dagger and
  sheath); BabelStone: page 28 (shield); Bearas: page 29 (map; Bibi
  Saint-Pol: front cover (bowl)
World Travel CD: cover (bottom right)

Illustrations:
William Band: pages 10, 28 (top), 31
Jeff Crosby: pages 12–13
Roman Goforth: page 27
Robert MacGregor: cover (map)

Library and Archives Canada Cataloguing in Publication

CIP available at Library and Archives Canada

Library of Congress Cataloging-in-Publication Data

Trade and commerce in the ancient world.
    p. cm. -- (Life in the ancient world)
  Includes index.
  ISBN 978-0-7787-1737-9 (reinforced library binding : alk. paper) -- ISBN 978-0-
7787-1744-7 (pbk. : alk. paper) -- ISBN 978-1-4271-8803-8 (electronic pdf) -- ISBN
978-1-4271-9644-6 (electronic html)
  1. Commerce--History. 2. International trade--History. I. Crabtree Publishing
Company. II. Title.

  HF357.T67 2012
  382--dc23

                                              2011029255

Crabtree Publishing Company

Printed in Canada/082011/MA20110714

www.crabtreebooks.com   1-800-387-7650

Published in Canada
Crabtree Publishing
616 Welland Ave.
St. Catharines, Ontario
L2M 5V6

Published in the United States
Crabtree Publishing
PMB 59051
350 Fifth Avenue, 59th Floor
New York, New York 10118

Published in the United Kingdom
Crabtree Publishing
Maritime House
Basin Road North, Hove
BN41 1WR

Published in Australia
Crabtree Publishing
3 Charles Street
Coburg North
VIC, 3058

Contents

4 Trade and Commerce in the Ancient World

6 Ancient China

8 Ancient Mesopotamia

10 Ancient Indus River Valley

12 Ancient Greece

14 Ancient Egypt

16 Ancient Africa

20 Ancient Mesoamerica

22 Ancient South America

24 Ancient Japan

26 Ancient Rome

28 Ancient Celts

30 Ancient Vikings

32 Glossary, Index, Websites, and Further Reading

Trade and Commerce in the Ancient World

Most historians agree that a civilization is a group of people that shares common languages, some form of writing, advanced technology and science, and systems of government and religion. The first known civilization developed in ancient Mesopotamia, in present-day Iraq, where the permanent settlements in the southern region of Sumer became important centers for trade. For the other ancient civilizations throughout Europe and Asia, trade became the catalyst for their prosperity and advancement, too.

Growth and Prosperity

The people within each civilization traded goods with each other, but the development of accessible trade routes made it possible to trade with peoples of other civilizations. Vast distances between major centers of commerce were traveled by pack animals on overland routes, or by ships along sea routes. Cities that were located along these routes grew rich as marketplaces were set up and services such as lodging were offered to weary travelers. The trade routes allowed people to trade for the raw materials and luxury goods specific to each ancient empire, such as the silk from China and the spices from south Asia. Not only did trade among empires result in increased wealth for each civilization, but the transmission of new inventions, languages, religious beliefs, and social customs also took place as people traveled from place to place.

The ruins of an ancient Roman market from the city of Leptis Magna still stand in present-day Libya. Leptis Magna was a leading city and major trading post of the Roman Empire.

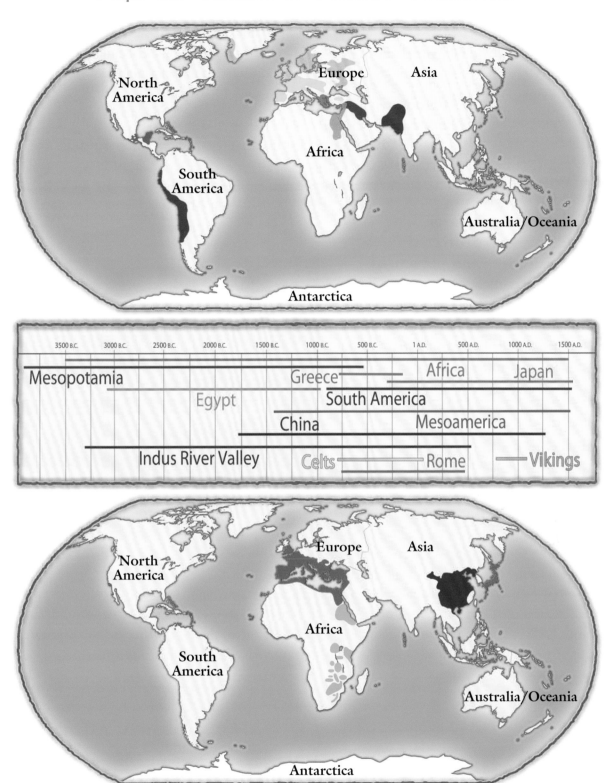

The period described as ancient history is usually defined as the time from first recorded history up to the Early Middle Ages, around 300 A.D. Some of the civilizations in this book begin well after the ancient period but are included because they were dominant early civilizations in their regions. The beginning and ending dates of early civilizations are often subject to debate. For the purposes of this book, the timelines begin with the first significant culture in a civilization and end with the change or disappearance of the civilization. The end was sometimes marked by an event such as invasion by another civilization, or simply by the gradual dispersion of people due to natural phenomena such as famine or earthquakes.

Ancient China

Ancient China was one of the most advanced civilizations the world has ever known. For most of its 7,000-year history, lack of easy land or sea routes stopped travelers from other parts of the world from visiting China. Tall mountains, large deserts, and vast seas protected the people from invaders and prevented outside traders from entering. This made China both an independent and prosperous society. The early Chinese people depended on farming and trading. Then, over many years, China developed a network of routes across Asia to trade its crops and goods. The development of using coins as money also made trade easier.

1766 B.C.–1271 A.D.

Fertile River Valleys

The Yellow and Yangzi rivers flooded their banks most years and left a rich, fertile topsoil, or silt, on the surrounding land that made planting and growing easy. Most Chinese were peasant farmers who grew crops on small plots of land. All family members were expected to work on these farms, which grew crops such as millet, rice, and wheat for people in the army and in the cities. Farmers used simple wooden or stone tools and most labor was done by hand. Farm animals were not common, so families often used their own waste as fertilizer. Painted clay pots were used to store the harvest.

Chinese farmers used oxen and water buffalo to pull plows made of iron to till the soil. Peasants in southern China planted rice shoots in flooded rice fields called paddies, which were built in terraces on the sides of mountains.

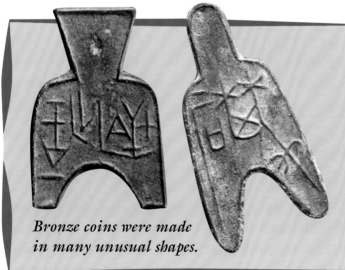

Bronze coins were made in many unusual shapes.

Money, Money, Money

The Chinese people used a system of coins, or currency, for buying goods as early as 2005 B.C. Shells, knives, and silk were the earliest forms of currency. During the Qin dynasty (221 B.C.– 206 B.C.), the emperor declared that coins should be standardized, or worth the same amount in every part of China. A common currency made it easier for people to trade with each other.

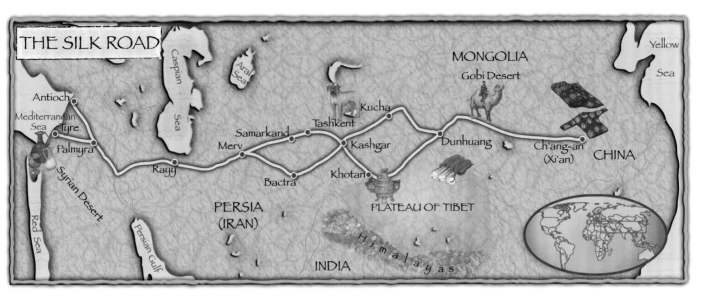

Map labels:

THE SILK ROAD

Caspian Sea · Aral Sea · Yellow Sea · MONGOLIA · Gobi Desert · Antioch · Mediterranean Sea · Tyre · Palmyra · Rayy · Samarkand · Merv · Tashkent · Kucha · Kashgar · Dunhuang · Ch'ang-an (Xi'an) · CHINA · Bactra · Khotan · PLATEAU OF TIBET · Syrian Desert · Red Sea · Persian Gulf · PERSIA (IRAN) · Himalayas · INDIA

The Chinese built a network of roads and canals to allow people to trade with each other. The most famous trade route was the Silk Road, which stretched from China across Asia to the Mediterranean Sea. Silk was a rare and valued fabric that ancient Chinese traded with other peoples. Large-scale silk production began in China as early as the Zhou dynasty (1122 B.C.–221 B.C.). Along the Silk Road, merchants traveled by camel across deserts to trade Chinese silk, tea, and spices for gold, silver, and precious stones from Central Asia.

Ancient Inventions

China grew from a collection of small farming villages into large cities, where markets and culture flourished. The ancient Chinese developed a system of writing so that people all over China could communicate with each other, making trade easier. Innovative inventions also helped spread trade across China. Many of ancient China's advances were adopted by peoples around the world and are still used today, such as paper and printing.

The Chinese invented the abacus, a counting tool that used rods and sliding beads to calculate sums for trading goods. Sometimes called "the world's first calculator," the abacus is still used in some parts of China.

Contact with Europeans

In 1206, a great ruler named Genghis Khan captured northern China. The Mongols opened China to greater trade with the rest of the world. In 1275, an Italian explorer named Marco Polo visited the emperor Kublai Khan. Amazed by the beautiful work of Chinese artisans and by China's many scientific and cultural advances, Marco Polo carried word of China's civilization back to Europe.

In 1644, the Manchu people ruled China until 1912. The Manchu closed off trade with other countries and banned foreign ships from China's harbors. These actions weakened China's economy. In 1912, the last emperor was dethroned. China became a democratic **republic**, then in 1949, a **communist** country. For many years, farming was the foundation of China's economy. However, population numbers soared above food production, and China faced famine and many economic crises. Economic reforms introduced in China in 1976 opened up trade within China as well as trade with Western countries. Today, China has the second largest economy in the world.

Ancient Mesopotamia

Historians refer to ancient Mesopotamia as "the birthplace of civilization" because it is the earliest known civilization. By 3800 B.C., people known as the Sumerians ruled southern Mesopotamia, and the permanent settlements there became a center of agriculture and trade, both for its citizens and for nomadic peoples from neighboring regions. Mesopotamia's economy was based on agriculture. Crop surpluses meant that people could trade food for other goods. Some people survived by trading their crafts, skills, or labor for food. Merchants and scribes emerged to keep track of transactions. Before long, trade spread among city-states.

The Rivers and Agriculture

The name Mesopotamia comes from a Greek word that means "land between two rivers"—in this case, the Tigris and Euphrates. Today, this area has become known as the Fertile Crescent. Both rivers provided drinking water, **irrigation** for fields, and transportation routes for trade. When the rivers flooded each year, they left minerals behind making the soil rich for farming. Some crops, such as dates and sesame, could be eaten or used to make products such as oil. Other crops, such as barley and wheat, could also be traded as raw materials. Irrigation plus the invention of the seed plow allowed for more crops to be grown and traded. In the south where there is little rain, farmers developed irrigation systems to bring water from the rivers to their crops before the annual floodwaters came. However, the irrigation process became a problem because it sometimes left too much salt in the soil. Eventually it poisoned the plants and the fields had to be abandoned. When there was no crop surplus, Mesopotamians could not trade for the objects they needed to make weapons and buildings. Over time, Mesopotamians learned to deal with the salt by leaving some land unplanted for a time to allow the soil to recover.

The Fertile Crescent was an area suitable for growing crops in the otherwise dry lands of the Middle East. The Tigris marks the eastern edge of the Fertile Crescent and is still an important river for agriculture today.

Trade

The need for materials drove city-states to trade with neighboring states. When building materials such as timber and stones were needed, they had to be brought in from the mountain areas. Metal **ores** and precious stones were also brought from the mountains to make tools, jewelry, and weapons. Traders led **caravans** between Mesopotamia and the Zagros and Taurus mountains, and even as far as Egypt to the west. Some merchants used the Euphrates and Tigris rivers to ship their wares downstream. Others used donkey carts to carry their goods.

Slave Labor

Most slaves were prisoners of war captured from outside Mesopotamia. Slavery was also a form of punishment for Mesopotamians who broke the law by **assaulting** family members. Free workers could volunteer themselves or their family members into slavery to repay debts. Once their services to their owners were complete, slaves could work at other jobs to earn money. They were allowed to own property and conduct business. Some slaves made enough money to purchase their freedom.

Spreading the Word

The Hittites were great traders and warriors from the north who conquered the Mesopotamian city of Babylon in 1595 B.C. Through trade, they spread the culture, laws, and ideas of Mesopotamia to other lands with whom they did business.

Money Matters

Mesopotamians originally traded through barter. Barter is a system in which one product or service is traded for another product or service of similar value. In time, bars of valuable metals, such as copper, silver, and gold were exchanged for other goods. Merchants measured these metals out in each transaction. The Mesopotamians were among the first people to use a number system for weights and measurements. It helped keep business fair and easy to understand for traders from different lands. In fact, the oldest standard of length in the world today is the foot, first established by the Sumerians in 2575 B.C.

As trade increased, it became more important to keep track of all these transactions. Traders employed scribes to record transactions in pictographs. This form of record-keeping eventually turned into a written language called cuneiform, one of the world's oldest known writing systems.

A stone tablet from the Babylonia region shows pictographs carved into it.

Caravans including animals loaded with goods, crossed deserts in search of trading partners.

Ancient Indus River Valley

Two of the world's greatest ancient civilizations began in the Indus River Valley, in what is now Pakistan. The earliest was the Harappans, who built highly advanced cities from 2600 B.C. to 1900 B.C. In 1750 B.C., the Aryans, a warrior people from the north, invaded the Indus River Valley and then spread across ancient India. The ancient Indus River Valley was a paradise for traders. By 2000 B.C., the Harappans were trading grain, cloth, and gems from China to Persia, or present-day Iran. Following in the Harappans' footsteps, the Aryans exchanged goods to the same peoples on the same routes.

3300 B.C.–550 A.D

The Bountiful Earth

Today, the Indus River Valley is a dry, barren area, but thousands of years ago, it was lush. Each spring, meltwater from the Himalaya Mountains and summer **monsoon** rains caused the Indus and Saraswati rivers to overflow. Muddy water, or silt, covered the **floodplains**, keeping the soil fertile.

Harappan farmers grew barley, wheat, melons, and dates. They also grew cotton, which they used to make cloth for clothing. The Harappans also herded sheep, goats, and a type of cattle called zebus on nearby pastures, and caught fish in the Arabian Sea. The Aryans were also farmers and grew rice and other grains on the plains alongside the Ganges River.

Caravans of elephants carried goods along trade routes. All the major Harappan towns and cities were along these routes. Later, the routes were used by Aryan traders as well.

Metals and Minerals

The Himalaya Mountains in the north were a source of flint, which the Harappans made into blades and other tools. Copper and tin were mined and used to make saws, axes, and chisels. Forests to the west provided wood for tool handles, as well as firewood. Even the plains of the Thar Desert to the east were a resource. The Harappans used gemstones found there, such as lapis lazuli and turquoise, in jewelry they traded with other peoples.

Overland Trade

Traders used pack animals, including two-humped camels, elephants, and carts pulled by bulls to carry goods overland. They traveled long distances over mountain routes through Afghanistan, Persia, and eastern China.

Valuable Goods

The Harappans exchanged grain, copper pots and pans, mirrors, elephant ivory, cotton cloth, lapis lazuli, shells, and ceramic jewelry for silver from Persia and Afghanistan, and gold and dried fish from Mesopotamia.

Sea Trade

Harappan boats laden with surplus, or extra, crops and other goods sailed up the Persian Gulf toward Persia and Mesopotamia, or modern-day Iraq. These month-long voyages were timed to take advantage of monsoon winds. Ships left Harappan ports between November and April, when the winds blew northeast. They returned between July and September, when winds blew southwest.

Money, Money, Money

For thousands of years, the people of the Indus River Valley and ancient India used a barter, or swapping, system, rather than money. Silver bar coins from Persia were first used in ancient India long after the Aryans were established. The coins made it easier to trade because all items had a standard value.

Exchanging Ideas

The Harappans were the first people to weave the fluffy heads, or bolls of a cotton plant, into thread. They passed this knowledge on as they traded with the Mesopotamians and Persians, and it spread around the world. The Harappans also learned new skills, such as how to make simple plows, called ards, from the Mesopotamians. Later, the ancient Indians began growing rice brought by Chinese traders. Rice then became a main crop of farmers.

Disaster Strikes

Historians believe that the Harappan civilization may have ended because of environmental changes. By 1800 B.C., the people had destroyed most of the forests, the Saraswati River dried up, and the Indus River changed its course. Farmland dried up. Towns were no longer on the riverbanks and therefore lost the income they received from trade. The shift also caused devastating floods. These changes altered the economy of the area and may have made the civilization decline.

Today, cotton textiles and clothing are still made in modern Pakistan and India and are exported around the world. Many small farming communities in India and Pakistan are located near the sites of ancient Harappan and Indian cities and villages. Farmers still use some of the technology developed thousands of years ago, including ox carts and pottery wheels.

An Ancient Unicorn

All Harappan trade goods had a pottery seal attached to them. Seals had writing and an image of an animal on them. Sometimes the animal was an elephant, a rhinoceros, or a bull, which represented gods. A unicorn was the most common image on seals. Some historians think that the unicorn was the symbol of the Harappan people or government. Around 1900 B.C., when the Harappan civilization started to decline, the unicorn image was no longer made on seals.

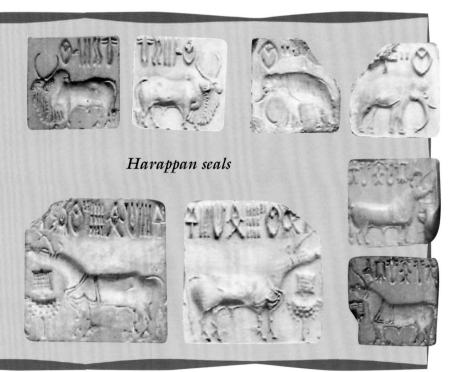

Harappan seals

Ancient Greece

Ancient Greece was not one country. It was a group of individual communities scattered along the rugged landscape of the Greek mainland and on about 170 islands in the Aegean Sea. Each community was separated from the next by either mountains or sea. The ancient Greeks developed a way of life that was inspired by their land, becoming expert sailors, traders, and warriors. Mountains and barren plains covered most of Greece so farmers struggled hard to produce crops. Lack of farmland was the main reason why Greeks established colonies around the Mediterranean Sea.

Call of the Sea

Most ancient Greek cities were built near the coast so shipping and fishing were easy. The Greeks panned the sea for salt, and fishers caught tuna fish, anchovies, and sardines. When a city did not have enough food, people moved to colonies. Colonies were useful trading posts for merchants to trade goods they produced, such as olive oil and minerals, for wheat, wood, and other items they needed.

Resources

The forests of northern Greece provided timber to the south where wood was scarce. Greece's rocky land provided minerals for tools and weapons, and marble and stone for buildings and sculptures. Mines near Athens were rich in silver, marble, iron, and lead. Slaves were forced to work these mines day and night for merchants to trade these precious items around the world.

800 B.C.–146 B.C.

Ships called triremes *carried Greeks to new lands to live, trade, and fight wars.*

Daily Work

Ancient Greek society depended on people doing different tasks. The wealthy lived a life of leisure, often serving in politics or debating philosophy. Many people were farmers, while others were teachers, merchants, sailors, metal workers, and marble workers. Most hard labor was done by slaves.

Slaves and Metics

Slaves were abandoned infants, prisoners of war, criminals, or individuals bought at market from the slave traders. A freedman was a slave who earned his freedom by buying it from his master. Other manual laborers were metics, who were foreigners, or people from other places. Sometimes metics became wealthy by saving the money they earned.

Super Markets

Food and goods were sold and traded in a central marketplace of a city, called the agora. Grain and goods imported from across the sea were shipped to the Athenian port at Piraeus, and then brought a short distance overland to the marketplace in Athens.

1. Local farmers and vendors hauled their wares in carts they pulled themselves or with a donkey.

2. The agora was like a modern day shopping mall that sold items such as food, clothing, housewares, pottery, and slaves.

3. Women could draw water from a well located in the agora.

4. After 500 B.C., most city-states had their own gold or silver coins, and decorated them with local gods or symbols. The silver Athenian coin displayed the goddess Athena on one side and an eagle on the other.

5. The agora was an important place in all Greek cities. Local artisans kept their workshops near the agora to attract shoppers.

6. The agora's central location within the city also made it a place where men could meet and discuss ideas and politics.

Ancient Egypt

Egypt's civilization is one of the oldest in human history. The first settlements grew on the banks of the Nile River about 7,000 years ago. In the fertile Nile soil, farmers grew food for the Egyptians, as well as merchants who sailed the Nile's waters and builders who constructed canals and cities on its banks. The pharaoh, or king, owned all the farmland and taxed everyone, from traders to craftsmen and farmers.

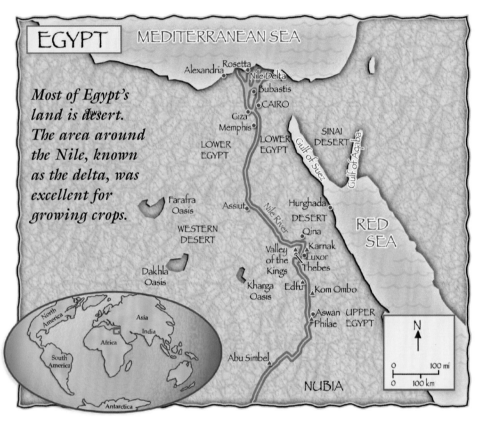

Most of Egypt's land is desert. The area around the Nile, known as the delta, was excellent for growing crops.

This mural painting shows an Egyptian couple harvesting crops.

The River Delta

The Nile is the longest river in the world. The triangle where the river meets the Mediterranean Sea is known as the Nile delta. Every year from July to October, rain caused the Nile to flood and leave muddy soil behind providing Egyptians with rich farmland. The river also supplied water for grazing pastures. A plant called papyrus grew in the river's marshes and was used to make paper and boats for fishing.

Agriculture

Egyptian farmers grew wheat, barley, peas, beans, onions, garlic, leeks, cucumbers, grapes, melons, pomegranates, figs, and dates to feed the growing population. They used the Nile's water to irrigate dry land. A network of irrigation canals supplied crops grown farthest away from the river with water.

During harvest time, all available workers, including soldiers, harvested the grain. With good irrigation, Egyptian farmers grew more grain than was needed to feed themselves, the army, and the workers who built the pharaoh's temples. The surplus seeds and grain were bartered for other goods with peoples to the south.

14

Bringing Water to the Soil

The Nile River flooded every summer. If flood waters were too low for several years in a row, it would be too dry to farm and there would be famine. Flooding forced farmers and villagers from their homes near the banks to higher ground. Workers built dikes to keep the river from flooding villages.

Big catch basins were built to trap water as the floods receded. Workers dug canals leading from these basins so the water could be used in fields located farther away. By law, every citizen had to maintain the irrigation system. The wealthy paid others to do their share.

Slavery

Ancient Egyptians kept slaves who were considered the property of their master. Most slaves were non-Egyptians captured in war. Slaves were forced to labor in the copper and gold mines of Sinai and Nubia. Other slaves were forced to fight in the Egyptian army or work for nobles.

Trade

Ships made of reed, papyrus, and wood sailed the Nile, carrying goods for trade. Egyptians traded objects crafted from gold, as well as papyrus for writing, with people who lived up the Nile and across the sea.

There were no coins or money. Merchants used a system called barter in which people traded one item they possessed for another they needed. They traded for wine and oil from the island of Crete, in the Mediterranean Sea. Timber, tin, and horses were purchased from the eastern part of the Egyptian Empire. Copper for making tools came from Sinai, a peninsula on the northern end of the Red Sea to Egypt's east. Salt, dates, reeds, and cattle came from the desert oases. Gold, copper, amethyst, and cattle came from Nubia, a desert to the south and an incense called myrrh came from Punt, a desert in East Africa.

Many still sail the Nile for enjoyment, transportation, and trade.

Egyptians used a tool called a **shaduf** *to lift water from the Nile to irrigate canals near fields.*

Sailing

Traffic was heavy on the Nile. Merchants, fishers, traders, stone haulers, and nobles all used the Nile to do their business. Egyptians constructed reed rafts for going through narrow canals and 200-foot (61-meter) long barges for hauling **obelisks**. They built boats to ferry people across the river. The wealthy relaxed on boats piloted by mariners on the Nile to catch the cooling breezes. Freighters carried grain up and down the river.

Ancient Africa

The histories of Africa's great empires and cultures, and how they influenced each other, are only just beginning to be understood. Ancient Africa was the world's richest source of gold and ivory. It also had many items other nations considered exotic, such as ebony, and leopard and zebra skins. Salt was also an important item for trade for many African civilizations. Merchants from Europe and Asia sailed to Africa to trade for these treasures. Eventually, European nations invaded, enslaving millions and stealing Africa's resources.

The Earliest Civilizations

About 4000 B.C., at the same time that ancient Egypt arose, the civilization of Nubia, a **rival** to ancient Egypt, was developing directly to the south. Many African civilizations emerged all over the continent, including the Aksumites, cultures from the Niger River Valley and the Swahili Coast, ancient Zimbabwe, and the empires of Benin, Ghana, Mali, and Songhai. Many great African civilizations traded with each other and with people from lands as far away as India and China. Africans also built great cities and became skilled farmers and **pastoral** herders.

Nubian Trade

Trade between Egypt and Nubia began as early as 4000 B.C. Nubian traders took precious stones and gold, stone for building, leather for making clothing and shoes, and dates for eating, to Egypt. In return, the Nubians received Egyptian linen, glass, and jewelry. Merchants from Babylonia, in present-day Iraq, the Indus River Valley, and ancient India sailed across the Red Sea to trade with the Nubians. They brought pottery, cotton cloth, perfume, wine, and glass to exchange for gold, ivory, and slaves.

The Nubians were the first civilization in the world to develop a large-scale iron **smelting** industry for producing metal goods. Much of their greatest artwork was made of iron. Nubian artisans also made priceless golden treasures, including the masks found in Egyptian pyramids and tombs.

Aksum Exports

The Aksumites set up extensive trade routes between Africa, India, and Arabia. The Aksumite seaport of Adulis on the Red Sea was busy with Greek, Roman, and Chinese ships. The foreign traders arrived with cotton, linen, and woolen cloth, gold and silver jewelry, bronze, tin, silver, and steel. These were exchanged for slaves, live monkeys and elephants, elephant tusks, rhinoceros horns, hippopotamus leather, tortoise shells, and musk from the civet cat for making perfume.

The Aksumites produced goods such as pottery and worked metal into objects they could use. They were a great trading nation, exporting goods, such as ivory and emeralds, and importing jewelry, fabrics, wine, and other items from India, Egypt, Greece, and Rome. Aksum began to decline around 600 A.D. when **Arab** traders took control of the Red Sea trade routes between Africa, Arabia, and India. Unable to trade, Aksum lost much of its wealth and the empire fell.

Nubian artisans crafted many leather goods, such as this canteen, to trade with the Egyptians.

Wall and door decorations were typical in Nubian homes. The decorations were made using materials found in nature.

Carthage

Around 800 B.C., traders from Phoenicia, in what is now Lebanon, colonized the coast of northern Africa. The Phoenicians were the greatest sea travelers and merchants of their time and they called their African trading center Carthage. By 600 B.C., Carthage was one of the world's biggest cities, with two ports and the largest marketplace in the Mediterranean. Carthage was destroyed by the Roman Empire after a series of three wars known as the Punic Wars. The wars ended in 146 B.C. when Rome broke through the city walls after a siege that lasted three years. The Romans burned the city to the ground and killed nearly all the inhabitants. To make sure that Carthage was destroyed forever, the Romans sold all surviving inhabitants into slavery and spread salt over the farmland so that crops could no longer be grown there.

The Swahili Coast

The Swahili Coast is a 1,500-mile (2,400-kilometer) stretch of coastline along the present-day East African countries of Kenya and Tanzania. It was a central area of trade between Africa and other countries, including Europe, Asia, and the Middle East, starting around 100 A.D. These early coastal communities in eastern Africa were centers for farming, fishing, and iron working. Over time, as trade in gold, ivory, and slaves increased, a sea-trading economy was established. The Swahili Coast is named after the Swahili language spoken by the people in the region. Over time, this African language adopted many Arabic and Persian words and became the language of trade.

Important Oil

Ancient peoples in western Africa began farming the oil from palm trees around 5000 B.C. The palm tree had many uses. Its wood and branches were used for building and its leaves for weaving into mats and baskets. Palm oil was used to fry food, and to make bread and candles. Most palm oil is still produced in western Africa today. It is a major ingredient in soaps, lotions, creams, and margarine.

The First Steel

Western African cultures began to produce steel from iron ore 2,000 years ago. The ability to make steel was the secret of African blacksmith castes, or groups, who were believed to possess magical knowledge. Europeans did not discover a reliable method of producing steel until the 1800s.

The First African Coins

The Aksumites were the first peoples to use coins as a form of money. Other civilizations used salt, gold dust, or iron bars as currency. The Aksumites made many different gold, silver, and bronze coins, and used them to pay for foreign goods.

Before coins, ancient Africans bartered, or traded, for items they needed.

Camel Caravans

Camels were first brought to northern Africa by Arab traders around 500 A.D. Two hundred years later, camels were transporting goods across the Sahara Desert. The camels could carry heavy loads and go up to nine days without water and weeks without food. Crossing the Sahara became less difficult, and trade with western Africa increased. Caravans of up to 1,000 camels, tied together head to tail, made the journey across the Sahara sands from the Sahel to northern and eastern Africa in less than 40 days. Along the way, the caravans stopped at posts set up at oases for water and food. Over time, many of the desert oases became markets and meeting places for caravan traders.

All the Sahel civilizations traded with the kingdoms of northern and northeastern Africa. They mainly traded salt and gold, but also slaves, pepper, leather, indigo, ivory, ostrich feathers, and beeswax. Caravans returning to Ghana, Mali, and Songhai from these areas brought back woven and decorated cloth, copper, and silver.

Camels can carry loads of up to 500 pounds (225 kg). The camel uses fat stored in its hump for energy. In ancient caravans, there was one camel driver for every six camels.

Silent Trading

Silent trading was a type of trading practiced by Sahel civilizations. Merchants brought their goods to a spot on the riverbank, beat on a drum to announce their arrival, then left. Buying merchants came to examine the goods and laid down as much gold as they thought the goods were worth. The sellers returned to check the payment. If it was acceptable, they took the gold and left the goods. If it was not enough, they left both. The buyers returned and added more gold in payment, again beating a drum to alert the sellers. This continued until the sellers were satisfied or the buyers had reached the highest amount they were willing to pay.

Trade with Ancient Zimbabwe

Ancient Zimbabwe was the busiest and largest trading kingdom in ancient southern Africa. It traded with other African regions, including Katanga in present-day Congo. Traders from ancient Zimbabwe met with merchants from Arabia, South Asia, and India at the bustling port city of Sofala, in present-day Mozambique. They traded mostly copper jewelry, leather, and gold for porcelain, ceramics, glass beads, and cloth.

Ancient African traders were attracted to the Sahara region, where salt was plentiful.

The Salt Trade

Salt was one of the most precious items of the ancient world. The Sahel civilizations gained great wealth by trading salt, which was used to preserve food. In the trading cities of western Africa, salt was worth its weight in gold. It was sold at markets in enormous chunks. The main salt mines were at Targhaza in the Sahara Desert. Salt was mined by slaves and prisoners, many of whom had to work in the salt mines until they died.

End of the Empires

War and invasion were common in ancient Africa. Attacks and invasions disrupted trade routes. Without the wealth from trade, many civilizations could not support large armies to defend themselves. Some African civilizations, such as the Nubian kingdom of Kush, survived for thousands of years. Others lasted only a few hundred years. The arrival of European explorers led to the breakdown of the last of the African empires.

European Exploration

Portuguese explorers first sailed down the west coast of Africa in the 1300s. They were looking for a trade route to India and China. By the 1400s, they were exploring many of the lands south of the Sahara Desert. The Europeans were stunned by the rich gold deposits there. They set up trade routes through the African kingdoms to obtain this precious metal.

The Slave Trade

Portuguese traders brought copper, guns and ammunition, horses, and iron tools to trading towns along the African coast to trade for African gold. They quickly learned that African slaves were highly valued by Arab traders living in Africa. By 1450, the Portuguese were trading thousands of slaves at ports along the African coast. The slave trade grew after North and South America were colonized in the 1500s. European plantations in those colonies needed a labor force to clear ground, build, and work on sugar plantations. Over the next 300 years, more than ten million Africans were captured and shipped to these plantations as slaves.

Europeans Colonize Africa

From the 1500s through the 1800s, England, Germany, Portugal, Italy, France, and Holland seized most of Africa and divided it among themselves. The European colonizers often plundered Africa's natural resources and destroyed many African monuments and historical treasures in their search for gold and land for farms and plantations. Africans resisted enslavement and European colonization. Many of these struggles, in which colonial governments and ways of life were toppled and replaced with African ones, continued until the late 1900s.

Ancient Mesoamerica

1400 B.C.–1521 A.D.

The first peoples arrived in Mesoamerica, or the land between North and South America, about 10,000 years ago. Around 1800 B.C., the Olmec, Maya, and Aztec peoples began to settle in small communities. As settlements grew larger, new methods of farming were developed to feed the growing population. People in different parts of Mesoamerica grew different crops, so trade between settlements was necessary.

Farmers

Most Mesoamericans were farmers. Farmers' lives revolved around maize, or corn. If maize grew, the people could eat. If maize did not grow, the people would starve. Farmers were required to grow more maize than they could use themselves. The extra maize was used to pay tribute to the ruler of their city-state. The ruler would advise farmers when to plant crops and he arranged religious rituals and **sacrifices** to gain the favor of the gods, so crops would be plentiful. When they were not working the land, farmers worked on construction in the city. Farmers were also required to fight in wars.

Chinampas were built by piling mud on a frame of woven reeds.

Floating Gardens

Marshy areas were too wet for milpa farming, so Mesoamericans built raised fields, or floating gardens, called *chinampas*. Soil was dug from the surrounding area and piled up to form the banks of a canal. Wooden stakes were hammered into the ground to reinforce the canal's banks. Trees were planted around the banks and their roots kept the sides of the canal from being washed away.

Farming in the Rainforests

Mesoamericans used a method called "slash and burn," or *milpa* farming, to clear rainforest land to grow crops. Farmers cut a tree's bark in a circle around the trunk to kill it. Branches were then cut off and left at the tree's base. After the tree dried out, a fire was set to burn away the vegetation. The ash from the burned trees and vegetation fertilized the ground and made the soil good for growing food.

Trade

Mesoamerican city-states could not survive on what they grew for themselves. Some regions that were good for growing certain crops needed to trade with other regions to get building materials for temples. Trade between neighbors was necessary for the city-states to flourish. In the Aztec city of Tenochtitlán, there were markets every five days where merchants sold food, weapons, and clothing. Some Aztec merchants, called *pochteca*, traveled great distances to trade textiles, clothing, and stone knives with other Mesoamerican peoples. Aztec merchants enjoyed status and wealth because traveling for trade was a difficult and dangerous job.

Delivering the Goods

Mesoamericans did not have the wheel, or pack animals such as oxen, horses, or donkeys. Food and household items that were being traded had to be carried over land using a backpack called a *tumpline*. A *tumpline* rested on a person's back and was secured to the forehead by a headband.

Mayan Math

Merchants used a counting system with three symbols to tally sums during trade. Math was also used to plan construction of buildings and in astronomy to help figure out dates and times.

Aztec workers stored amaranth grain in large vessels that were used to carry the grain to markets.

Decline

Archaeologists know that some Mesoamerican cities were abandoned or destroyed. They do not know the reason why. Some think the land surrounding the cities was over farmed and could no longer grow crops to feed the population, forcing the people to move. Others believe the cities were attacked by invaders or even by rebels within the cities. The Aztecs, the last remaining empire of Mesoamerica, was destroyed when Spanish explorer Hernán Cortés defeated them in 1521 in the name of Spain.

Money Grown on Trees

Cocoa beans, which come from pods harvested from the cacao tree, were used as money by the Maya and the Aztecs. Cocoa beans were valuable because they were difficult to grow. The delicate cacao trees grew only in shady areas with high humidity. Once allowed to dry in the sun, the valuable beans were easy to carry, and so were used as money. They were also ground and used in a drink in religious ceremonies.

Ancient South America

Many of the ancient South American civilizations—the Chavin, the Moche, the Nazca, the Tiahuanaco, the Chimú, and the powerful Incas—developed in what is now known as the country of Peru. Seasonal floods in the river valleys made the soil rich for growing food. The Andes Mountains were plentiful with other resources that people used to improve their way of life, such as the llama and deposits of precious metals.

Surviving in South America

Life in the Andes was not easy. Mountain villages were shaken by earthquakes and volcanic eruptions, because the Andes range lies on a **fault line**. Life was even harder in parts of the continent where food could not be grown, such as on the dry coasts. Rainforests in the middle of the continent were difficult to clear because people did not have iron tools. The marshy mangrove swamps in the north were also unsuitable for farming because the soil was too wet.

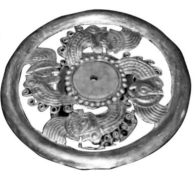

Gold was hammered into thin plates and sculpted to be used for decorating clothing, utensils, and rulers' palaces.

Harvests from the Land and Sea

The ancient Andeans grew crops on the fertile plains, or *puna*, of the mountains. Ancient Andeans also used stone tools to dig at mountain deposits of gold and silver. Gold nuggets, found in the Andes and in mountain streams, were melted down and used to make various items.

The most important animal for people in the Andes was the llama, which was **domesticated** around 1000 B.C. The llama was used to carry goods along the steep mountain paths. Llama wool was spun into yarn for blankets and clothing, while llama meat, considered a delicacy, was eaten by the wealthy. Llamas were also sacrificed in religious ceremonies.

The first Andeans raised guinea pigs for their meat, and alpacas for their wool. On the coast, whales, sea lions, and fish were hunted for food. In the rainforest, people hunted animals and birds. They made colorful headdresses with feathers taken from parrots.

Terrace Farming

The steep slopes of the Andes were difficult to farm. Around 6000 B.C., the Andean people started to cut wide, flat steps into the mountains, creating terraces for planting crops. Long canals were built to channel water from mountain rivers and streams to the terraced fields. These new farming methods allowed people to grow large amounts and varieties of food, including maize, potatoes, tomatoes, peanuts, chilies, and quinoa, a cereal grain. They also grew cotton to make clothing.

The Allyus

The Sapa Inca, or emperor, controlled all of the land in the empire. Plots of land called *allyus* were given to groups of families. The families of an *allyu* worked together to farm the land. Men caught fish and other seafood on the coasts. Women either helped in the fields or wove textiles that were worn, traded, or buried with the dead. Artisans within the *allyu* made pottery vessels from clay, and gold ornaments that were worn by the ruling class. The Incas developed their large empire by taking over land that was lived on by other peoples. Conquered peoples were taught Inca farming and weaving techniques, and paid taxes to the emperor as the Incas did.

Hand looms are still used today to weave textiles.

Dividing the Land

Each Inca community was divided into three parts. Harvests from one part were distributed among the people so that everyone was fed. Crops from the other two portions of farmland were given to nobles and administrators. Llama and alpaca herds were divided among the people in the same way. Every family received all the food, housing, and wool it needed. As payment, people had to pay taxes to the government in the form of either labor or goods.

Trade

Ancient South Americans did not use money. People bartered with each other for the things they needed, such as food, tools, and cloth. The Inca work force was so well organized that they produced all that they needed and did not have to trade with peoples outside their empire.

The Incas built roads that criss-crossed the Andes so they could travel through the mountains. The road network was called the Royal Road, and eventually ran the length of the Inca empire, covering over 14,000 miles (22,500 km). Llamas were used as pack animals to carry goods between communities. Llamas carried up to 70 pounds (32 kg) of goods loaded in baskets on their backs. Caravans traveled on stone roads first built by earlier civilizations. The Incas traded with the indigenous peoples of the Amazon rainforest, swapping bronze tools and gold for monkeys and colorful feathers.

Surviving Customs

The ancient Andeans developed ways of living that were different from other civilizations. Many of their innovations are still a part of life in South America today. Today, millions of indigenous people live in the Andean highlands. They farm on terraces growing corn, potatoes, and peppers as their ancestors did. Many drink *chicha* and roast guinea pigs for special occasions. Peasant women weave cloth from llama wool, using the same designs as the ancient South Americans.

Ancient Foods

More than half of the types of fruits and vegetables we eat were cultivated by ancient Andean farmers. Potatoes, grown on terraces in the Andes thousands of years ago, were brought back to Europe by Spanish explorers in 1565. The potato is now one of the most popular crops in the world. Other foods that originally came from ancient South America are sweet potatoes, corn, squash, many types of beans, pineapple, tomatoes, peppers, strawberries, and peanuts.

Ancient Japan

300 B.C.–1582 A.D.

People first settled on the islands that make up Japan 30,000 years ago. The ancient Japanese lived in the mountain valleys and on the coastal plains of the islands. Rice grown in wet paddies was their most successful crop, so much so that by 100 B.C. there was extra rice for trade with other civilizations. Additional trade goods were made from rice, such as sake, or rice wine, and vinegar. Rice became so important to Japan's economy that it was used as money for more than 1,000 years.

Valuable Rice

The ancient Japanese planted rice in waterlogged fields between April and May. In early June, a rainy season, called *tsuyu*, began. *Tsuyu* rains provided the water that food crops, like rice, needed to grow.

In ancient Japan, a person's wealth was measured in *kokus*. One *koku* was 47 gallons (180 liters) of rice. Peasant taxes were charged in rice, and the government paid its high-ranking workers with it. Rice was eaten with every meal. It was also used to make sake, flour, and vinegar. Stalks of rice plants were used to make floor mats, ropes, and sandals.

Most people in ancient Japan lived in small farming communities on land ruled by clans or powerful landowners. Working families shared plots of land and worked together to plant and harvest crops. Many of the ruling families competed for power and had private armies.

rice

Rice farming became so important in ancient Japan that it changed the way people lived, worked, and were governed.

Trade with China and Korea

Around 2000 B.C., a small amount of trade between Japan and China began when Chinese traders sailed across the East China Sea to Japan in wooden canoes. Trade increased greatly after 57 A.D., when Japanese **envoys** were sent to Korea and China. Both the ancient Koreans and the Chinese were interested in Japanese silk, which was used to make beautiful clothing, such as kimonos, or robes. Peasants made silk by keeping silk worms under the roofs of their homes. The worms spun silk cocoons that were later harvested and woven into fabric.

Volcanic eruptions in Japan left behind lava rich with gold, zinc, and copper. The ancient Koreans also traded iron and bronze tools in exchange for gold and rice from Japan. The ancient Chinese traded bronze mirrors, bells, swords, and spearheads for gold mined in Japanese mountains, as well as rice.

silk worm cocoons

Chinese Influence

People in ancient Japan traded with people from ancient Persia, India, China, and Korea. As trade between the nations grew, the Japanese began to borrow some of the traditions of these other cultures. The Japanese adopted Chinese styles of writing, artwork, and government until 894 A.D. After that, the people of ancient Japan changed the Chinese customs to fit with their own ideas and way of life.

Ships arrived at the port town Naniwa to unload trade goods onto barges that carried them across the city via canals.

Trading Groups

Trade with foreign countries was seen as a way to get wealthy. In 1185, rich artisans established trading groups called zas. Each za in a lord's territory traded one product, such as sake. The zas could charge whatever they liked for their products since there was no competition with other traders. The merchants and warlords became very wealthy as trade with other nations continued.

Japanese Coins

The ancient Japanese made purchases using quantities of rice rather than money. The first Japanese coins were made by the Yamato government in 708 A.D. The coins were round and had square holes in the center so they could be threaded onto string-like beads. At first, coins were made from copper and silver but were later made from copper only. The coins were not widely used because the government had difficulty getting them to isolated villages. The Japanese people went back to using rice instead of coins to pay for things.

European Contact

Europeans first landed in Japan in 1543, when shipwrecked Portuguese soldiers washed up on Japan's shores. Japanese merchants eagerly began trading with the Portuguese for their guns. In 1600, Dutch ships arrived at Kyushu and started to trade with the Japanese. Holland and Japan continued to trade for 250 years.

Retreat into Isolation

As trade between Japan and Europe opened up, Japan began to change. European traders brought their own customs, threatening Japanese traditions and beliefs. In the 1630s, the Japanese government banned most foreign trade. European ships were no longer allowed to dock at Japanese ports, except for a few Dutch ships. Japan's isolation from western countries lasted 251 years when in 1853, the Japanese agreed to a **treaty** proposed by the U.S. president, and two ports were opened to the Americans. Several years later, Japan's isolation had finally ended.

Ancient Rome

The ancient city of Rome spread out over seven hills along the Tiber River in what is now central Italy. It grew from a collection of farming villages to become the birthplace of a massive empire that stretched from Britain in the west to North Africa in the south and Asia in the east. Fertile farmlands in Egypt and North Africa provided food for a vast trading empire, and Rome was its center. Rome's shops displayed ostrich feathers from Egypt, wine from Portugal, cotton and silk from India and China, marble from North Africa, and fish from the Black Sea.

753 B.C.– 476 A.D.

Farming the Hills and Valleys

The seven steep hills of Rome are located fifteen miles (24 km) from the Mediterranean Sea. In ancient times, the hills were surrounded by marshy valleys. The land of ancient Rome had fertile soil for farming, mild weather, and plenty of rainfall. Winters were wet and mild and the summers were hot and dry. On the hillsides, Romans grew apples, pears, plums, and quince, as well as olives for making oil and grapes for making wine. Farmers raised sheep and goats and hunters caught wild boar and hare.

Climate

The Tiber River began in the Apennine Mountains and flowed through Rome. The river provided water for crops to grow on its fertile banks. The Tiber River emptied into the Mediterranean Sea. Romans used the river as a transportation route for trading, conquering, and spreading their culture. Near Rome there were forests of timber for building and shipmaking. Stone for making concrete to construct temples, amphitheaters, or vast outdoor arenas, and **aqueducts** was also plentiful.

Making a Living

Rome's ideal location and climate made it attractive to waves of settlers who ruled for a time, were defeated, and replaced by newcomers. Each group influenced the next through the religion, language, or culture it left behind. The streets of Rome were busy with traders and shoppers. Shops sold perfume, paint, rope, books, and herbs. Carpenters, butchers, harness makers, and stonecutters all set up shops in Rome's streets. Cargoes of marble, wood, granite, and brick from the colonies were unloaded at the seaport of Ostia and shipped up the Tiber to the city. Olive oil used for lamps, cooking, and in soap, was Rome's most important product.

Barter and Currency

Early Romans used a system of trade where cattle were exchanged for goods such as furniture, armor, or horses. The Latin word for money, *pecunia*, comes from *pecus*, the word for cattle. Romans bartered with cattle until 268 B.C. when the first coins were made in silver and bronze.

Coins had a set value and made trading across the empire easier.

Rural scene on an ancient farm

The Salt Road

Salt was so valuable to ancient peoples that it was used as a trade item and a form of payment. Salt was needed for preserving meat and fish before it rotted in the hot weather. The Roman government controlled the production of salt and kept the price low. Salt was collected from the sea or dug from underground mines throughout the empire. Roman **legionaries** were paid their wages, or salary, in salt. The Latin word for salt is *salaria*.

Bread and Circuses

Life in Roman cities was not always easy. When the Roman army returned from wars, they brought back prisoners as slaves from the colonies. Slaves replaced **plebeians** in many jobs, making it hard for plebeians to earn a living. Roman soldiers often returned home from battle to find their farms in ruins because no one had looked after them, and were forced to move to the city. In 41 A.D., during the reign of Claudius, Rome's poor and hungry were given government charity. They received free grain and admission to the circuses or theaters.

Slaving Away in Rome

The lowest class in Rome were slaves. Slaves were usually captured in war and had no rights in society. They worked for no pay and little food until they were too sick or old to work and were then abandoned. Those who did construction or dug mines had it the worst.

Troubles Within

Hundreds of thousands of people lived in Rome, most of them in crowded slums. A housing shortage, along with crime in the streets and soaring rents, meant that the ordinary person lived a life of misery. Unemployment was a serious problem. Things became worse when farm families flooded into the city. Food brought in from the colonies was sold at lower prices than the crops grown around Rome, so farmers did not make enough to survive. The economy was further weakened when returning soldiers brought the **plague** to Rome in 167 A.D. The plague killed about 2,000 people a day. With poor and weak rulers, Romans lost faith in their government and empire.

The End is Near

The Roman empire lasted for 1,500 years. Its influence and power spread through half the world. The end of the empire came in 476 A.D. after years of poor government, disease, and invasions by neighboring peoples. The once great Roman empire was no more.

Mercury: God of Merchants

Mercury was the Roman god of merchants. In statues and art, he was often shown holding a purse, because he was thought to help people in business. Mercury wore winged sandals or a winged hat to help speed him on his errands. The Romans honored him with a festival held on May 15. Named after the fast-moving Roman god, the planet Mercury orbits the sun more quickly than any of the other planets in the solar system.

Ancient Celts

The Celtic economy was based on agriculture, raising livestock, and trading. As the Celts expanded across Europe around 400 B.C., they took control of mines and other resources.

Agriculture

Most Celtic families raised their own animals, such as cows and pigs, for meat and skins. Families also grew vegetables, wheat, barley, and oats. The Celts used iron plowshares to work the fields. Plowshares are metal blades that cut loose the top layer of soil that is being cultivated, or prepared, for farming. The use of the iron plowshare made it easier to plow the heavy clay soil.

Mining

Salt was one of the Celts' most important trade goods. Salt was valuable in ancient times because it was used to preserve meat and fish, or stop them from rotting. One of Europe's largest salt mines was in the early Celtic settlement of Hallstatt, in Austria. The Celts dug deep shafts, or narrow passages, into the mountains to reach the salt. Tin was another valuable mining product of ancient Europe. Tin was needed to make a metal alloy called bronze, from which tools and other objects were crafted.

Desirable Goods

The Celts produced many goods that other ancient cultures wanted. The Celts traded salted fish, wool and woolen cloth, leather goods, helmets, and armor. Celtic ironwork was the finest in the ancient world, and their weapons and tools were prized trade items. With the wealth they acquired through trade, the Celts bought many precious goods, including wine and bronze wine goblets from Greece, silk from China, and glass beads from Egypt.

The Celts were the most advanced metalworkers in the ancient world. They used their skills to make tools for farming and mining, as well as weapons and armor.

The Conquest of Gaul

When the Romans met the Celts living in France, they called them the Gauls. Julius Caesar battled a Celtic group called the Helvetii to keep them from migrating westwards into France. After defeating the Celts, Caesar decided to conquer the rest of Gaul so that Rome could control the major trade routes for amber and tin. In 52 B.C., led by a Celtic chieftain named Vercingetorix, the Celts made a final stand against the Romans at a hillfort in France. The Romans surrounded the fortress, and the people inside slowly starved to death.

Vercingetorix

England

In 43 A.D., Claudius, the Roman emperor, ordered the invasion of England. His army quickly conquered the Celtic groups of southeast England. Some Celts welcomed Roman innovations and the building of new towns and roads after the conquest. Many druids fled into present-day Wales to avoid being captured and killed by the Romans. Most Celts in England took on the Roman way of life, languages, and religion. In other areas, such as Ireland, Celtic laws, languages, and oral histories continued to survive.

Scotland and Ireland

The Romans moved steadily northward through Europe, conquering Celtic groups as they went. The Romans never managed to conquer the Celts in the highlands of Scotland or in Ireland. The Celtic culture in Ireland remained intact well into the 400s A.D. when Christianity was introduced to the Celts. Christianity follows the teachings of Jesus Christ, believed to be the son of God. Many Celts **converted** to Christianity, but adapted some of their way of life into their new religious beliefs.

Celtic Crosses

Hundreds of stone crosses were raised in Ireland and Scotland by Celtic Christians. The crosses combined a circle, the Celtic symbol for the moon, and the Christian cross. The designs on the crosses, such as spirals, keys, and knot work, were copied from those used in Celtic metalwork.

Trade Routes

The Celts controlled many important trade routes in Europe. The Danube River was the major trade route for goods between Celtic lands and the Mediterranean. A group of Celts in Bohemia controlled the Amber Road, the main trade route for amber. Amber is a semi-precious stone formed from tree resin, or sap, that dried out millions of years ago. Amber was plentiful in the area known today as the Balkans. The Celts also used the Amber Road to trade other goods with the ancient Greeks, who were one of the Celts' most important trading partners. Celtic traders from the Alps traveled through difficult mountain passes to reach the Greek trading city of Massalia, which is today the French city of Marseilles.

Alpine Life

The **lowlands** had large forests of oak and beech, and a variety of birds for hunting. The grasslands teemed with European bison and wild boars, which the Celts hunted for food. Boars were a catch prized by Celtic hunters because they were regarded as sacred animals. In the mountains, chamois, a horned antelope, was hunted for its hide, which was made into fine leather. Highland meadows, covered with grasses and poppies, lay between mountain peaks and were ideal food for grazing cattle and goats.

A Varied Climate

Some Celts gradually migrated from the Danube and the Alpine lowlands to the Po Valley in Italy. Others settled in central Europe in what is now Moravia, Slovakia, and Hungary, where the winters were cold. There, a lot of rain fell in the lowlands and valleys, and snow fell in the mountains. The summers were cool, but often sunny. Grains, such as oats, rye, and barley, grew well in this climate. The Celts moved south into what is now northern Spain, where there were mild winters and long, hot summers. Peas, beans, and wheat were major crop plants, and fruits, such as plums, were collected in the wild.

Celtic Currency

When the Celts began to trade with other civilizations, they used iron bars and sword-shaped iron pieces as money. The first Celtic coins were made in 320 B.C. These were replicas of gold Greek coins and often depicted images of horses, the Celts' favorite animal in art, and wild boars. The Celts made coins from copper, silver, gold, and tin.

This Celtic coin depicts a horse.

The Amber Road was the major transport route of amber, an important raw material to the Celts.

Germans

Slavs

Roman Empire

chamois

Ancient Vikings

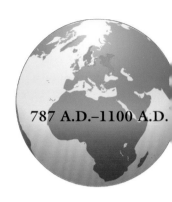

787 A.D.–1100 A.D.

During the Viking Age, from 787 A.D. to about 1000 A.D., the Vikings lived in Norway, Sweden, and Denmark, which make up the region of Scandinavia. Most early Vikings supported themselves and their families by farming and fishing. Scandinavia had little suitable land for farming, so the Vikings sailed the cold and stormy oceans in search of new lands to settle. Through their travels, raids, and conquests, the Vikings gained huge wealth and became the greatest international traders of their time.

Trading Towns

The Vikings held small marketplaces and trade fairs in Scandinavia. Among themselves, the Vikings traded meat and salted fish, livestock, wine, woven cloth, jewelry, pottery, glass, weapons, and slaves.

As Viking trade increased, some Viking marketplaces grew into major trading centers. The largest ones were Birka in Sweden, Hedeby in Denmark, Dublin in Ireland, and Jorvik in England. The trading towns were located on the coasts or on rivers that Viking ships could easily sail to. Traders from as far away as China came to these towns to trade with the Vikings.

Valuable Silver

Silver was one of the Vikings' most prized items. The Vikings in Russia set up a trade route that ran southward to Baghdad in modern-day Iraq. Viking goods, such as slaves, furs, and honey, were exchanged in Baghdad for silver coins, known as dirhems.

Looking for Luxuries

The Vikings began to trade with other countries to supply their chieftains with luxury goods, such as silver jewelry. The chieftains used these items to flaunt their wealth and to reward their followers.

The Vikings traded leather, walrus ivory, slaves, and foods, such as grains for making beer and breads. Furs from bears, otters, foxes, and minks were also popular items for trade. In return for these goods, Vikings received silks from China, spices from India, wine from France, glass and pottery from Germany, and tin from England. Every year, Viking traders sailed on ships laden with cargo to the large trading cities of Rome and Constantinople, which is modern-day Istanbul, in Turkey.

Settling in Greenland

Erik the Red discovered Greenland. Although most of it was Arctic tundra, and the coastline was covered with enormous glaciers, he called it Greenland to convince the Vikings in Iceland to settle there. The new settlers of Greenland fished and hunted polar bears, caribou, seals, and whales. They established a trade route to Norway, and traded salted fish and polar bear furs for tools, timber, and honey. The Vikings in Greenland lived quietly until the 1400s, when they suddenly disappeared. Historians do not know why, but some believe the disappearance was due to the **Inuit** peoples moving south from the Arctic and competing for territory.

Leif Erikson

Discovering North America

In 1000 A.D., Leif Erikson sailed from Greenland to explore farther west and discovered the island of Newfoundland, in Canada. Leif also found a forested land, which he named Vinland for the grapevines growing there. The Vikings tried to establish permanent bases there but were driven out by the indigenous peoples. The Vikings eventually abandoned their settlement and returned to Greenland.

Conquering the Slavs

When the Swedish Vikings wanted more land and new trade routes, they traveled eastward along rivers to what is now Russia. The area was the home of a group of farming people called the Slavs. Swedish Viking warriors invaded this land around 800 A.D., and made the Slavs build towns and roads, or sold them as slaves.

Russia had valuable natural resources. The Vikings trapped many native animals for their furs, such as bears, otters, and mink. The wide rivers allowed cargo ships to easily transport these prized furs and other trade goods.

The English Vikings

The Danish Vikings began to invade England after 850 A.D. because of the country's large amount of fertile farmland, dense forest, and supplies of copper and iron. After landing on the northeast coast of England, bands of Vikings on horseback rode across the country, attacking towns and cities as they went. They soon conquered all of the north and east of England. Eventually, Viking settlers developed the city of Jorvik into a major trading town.

Viking Slaves

Slaves, the lowest class in Viking society, were not free people. Some were people captured in Viking raids, and others were Vikings who had committed serious crimes, or had debts they could not pay. Each chieftain had about 30 slaves, and kings had more. Slaves had to obey their masters at all times and were often harshly treated. It was not a crime for a Viking to kill his own slave, but if he killed another Viking's slave, he had to pay for a new one.

Founders of the Modern World

The Vikings developed the economies of many European countries by building large trading towns across Europe. Viking traders were able to reach the trading towns by traveling over land on trade routes that stretched from modern-day Russia to China. The Vikings also founded many major cities, including Dublin in Ireland, Kiev in Ukraine, and Sicily in Italy.

The Viking Age ended about 1,000 years ago, but the Vikings have not been forgotten. Their lives of adventure, travel, and trade are recalled in the words we use, in entertainment, in the history of several of the world's greatest cities, and in our government and legal systems.

Viking Coins

Early Vikings did not use coins to pay for goods. Instead, most used the barter system, whereby a person exchanged goods or work for other goods that he or she wanted. Wealthy Vikings often paid for their goods with silver. Traders carried scales to weigh silver bars, coins, and jewelry because the value of the item was based on the weight of the silver in it. Once Vikings had settled in other lands, they made copies of those nations' coins to use.

Children born to slave women became the property of the woman's owner.

Glossary

aqueduct A channel for carrying fresh water

Arab A group of people originally from the Arabian peninsula

assaulting Violently attacking someone

caravan A group of merchants or other people traveling together on a long journey

city-state An independent city, usually walled for defense, and the surrounding towns and villages that depend upon it for defense

communist A person who believes in a system of government in which factories, farms, and other property are owned by everyone in common

convert To change religion

domesticate To train an animal to live with humans

emperor A ruler of a country or group of countries

envoy A person who is sent by one government or ruler to meet with another government or ruler

fault line A line of weakness in the Earth's crust

floodplains Flat areas next to a river that frequently flood

Inuit A member of a group of indigenous peoples living in the northern regions of North America

irrigation The process of supplying water to dry land using ditches, streams, or pipes

legionaries Ordinary foot soldiers in ancient Rome

lowland An area of low, flat land

monsoon Winds that bring heavy rain to south Asia

nomadic Moving from place to place

obelisks Columns, or shafts with four sides that usually come to a point at the top and are sometimes engraved or carved

ore A rock that contains minerals, such as copper and iron, that are used to make metals

pastoral Relating to the country or country life

plague A serious and deadly disease that is often spread to humans by infected fleas and carried by rats

plebeians Poor ancient Romans who were uneducated and did not own land

republic A state or system of government where power rests with citizens who vote for their leaders

rival An enemy or competitor

sacrifice An offering to a god or a goddess

scribes People who make a living by copying or recording text

smelt The process of removing metals from rock by using extreme heat

treaty An agreement made between one or more nations or rulers

Index

Africa 16–19, 26
agora 13
Amber Road 29
Andes mountains 22, 23
Arabia 16, 18
Aryans 10
Aztec 20, 21
barter 9, 11, 15, 17, 23, 26, 31
caravans 9, 10, 18, 23
Carthage 17
Celts 28–29
China 6–7, 10, 11, 16, 19, 24, 25, 26, 28, 30
cocoa beans 20
coins 6, 11, 13, 15, 17, 25, 26, 29, 30, 31
Egypt 14–15, 16, 26, 28
farming 6, 7, 8, 10, 11, 12, 14, 15, 16, 17, 19, 20, 21, 22, 23, 24, 26, 28, 29, 30
Fertile Crescent 8
gods and goddesses 11, 13, 20, 27
Greece 12–13, 16, 28, 29
Harappans 10, 11
Inca 22, 23
India 10, 11, 16, 18, 19, 24, 26, 30
Indus River Valley 10–11
irrigation 8, 14
Japan 24–25
llamas 22, 23
maize 20, 22
Manchu 7
markets 7, 12, 17, 18, 20, 30
Maya 20, 21
merchants 7, 8, 9, 12, 14, 15, 16, 17, 18, 20, 21, 25
Mercury 27
Mesoamerica 20–21
Mesopotamia 8–9, 11
metals 6, 7, 9, 10, 11, 12, 15, 16 17, 18, 19, 22, 23, 24, 25, 28, 30, 31
Nile River 14–15
Persia 10, 11, 24
Peru 22
Red Sea 16
rice 6, 10, 11, 24, 25
Rome 16, 17, 26–27, 28, 30
Royal Road 23
salt 17, 18, 27, 28
scribes 8, 9
silent trading 18
silk 6, 7, 24, 28, 30
Silk Road 7
slaves 9, 12, 13, 15, 17, 18, 19, 27, 30, 31
Sumerians 8
terraces 6, 23
tools 6, 9, 10, 12, 15, 19, 22, 23, 28, 30
Vikings 30–31
Yellow River 6
Yangzi River 6
za 25

Websites

www.bbc.co.uk/history/ancient/
 Amazing images highlight in-depth looks into ancient cultures.

www.pbs.org/wgbh/nova/ancient/
 Interactive videos take readers through ancient civilizations.

www.archaeolink.com/ancient_trade_routes.htm
 Learn about the trade routes between ancient civilizations.

www.archaeolink.com/amazing_worlds_of_archaeology1.htm
 This site provides links to sites with archaeological information.

Further Reading

Great Minds of Ancient Science and Math series, Enslow Publishers 2010

True Books: Ancient Civilizations series, Children's Press 2010

Biography from Ancient Civilizations: Legends, Folklore, and Stories of Ancient Worlds series, Mitchell Lane Publishers 2009

Ancient and Medieval People series, Benchmark books 2009